NATIONAL GEOGRAPHIC

Watermelons

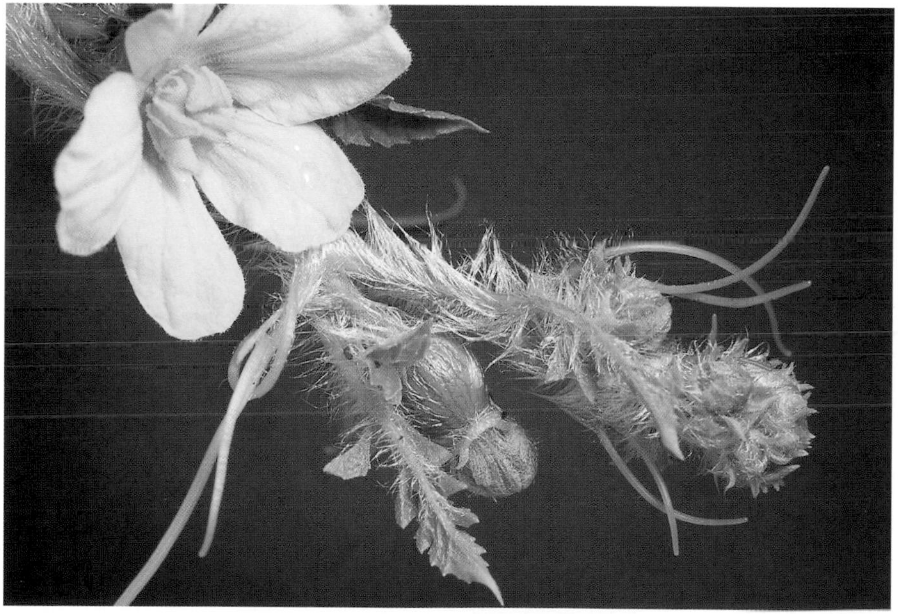

Terry O'Brady

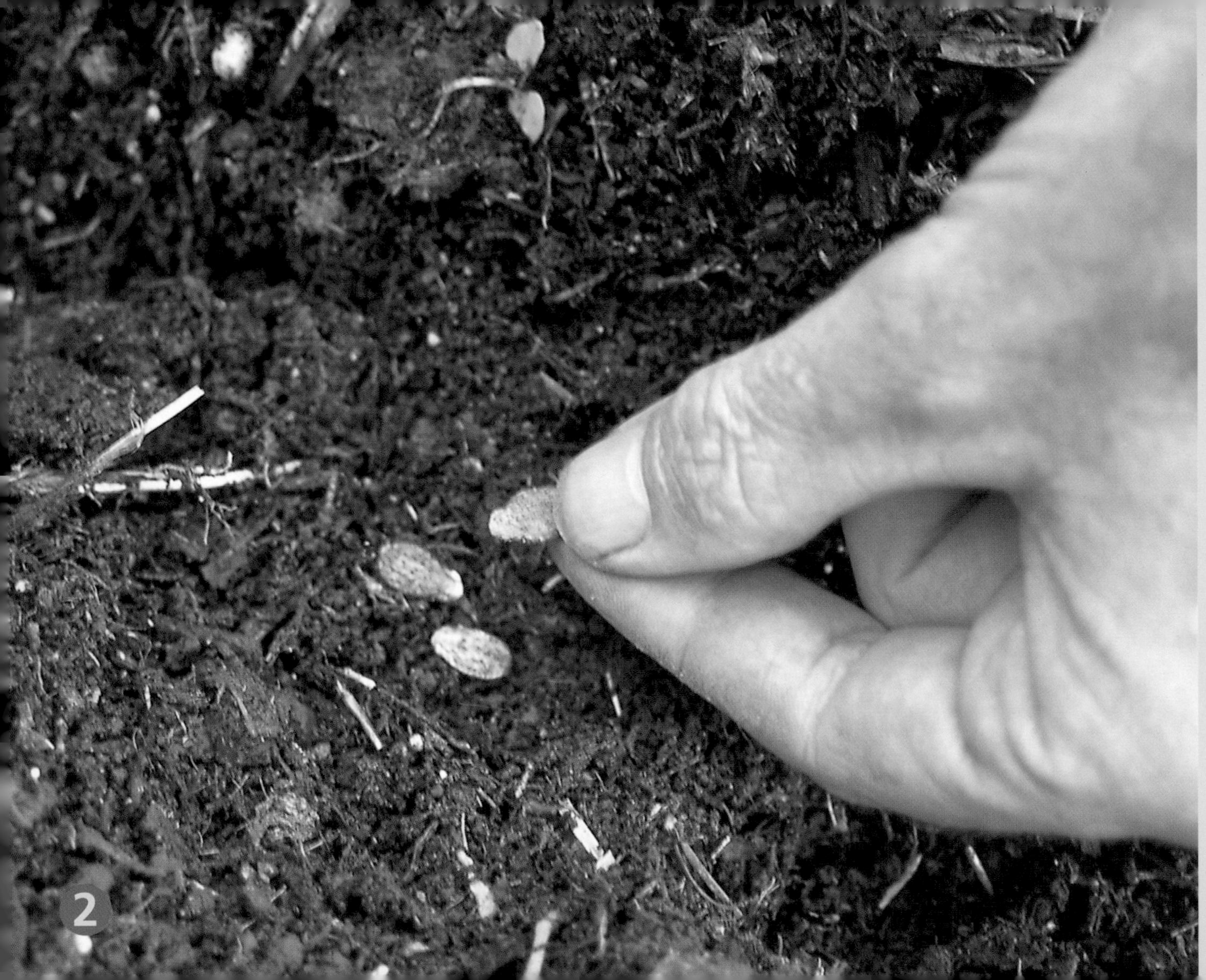
2

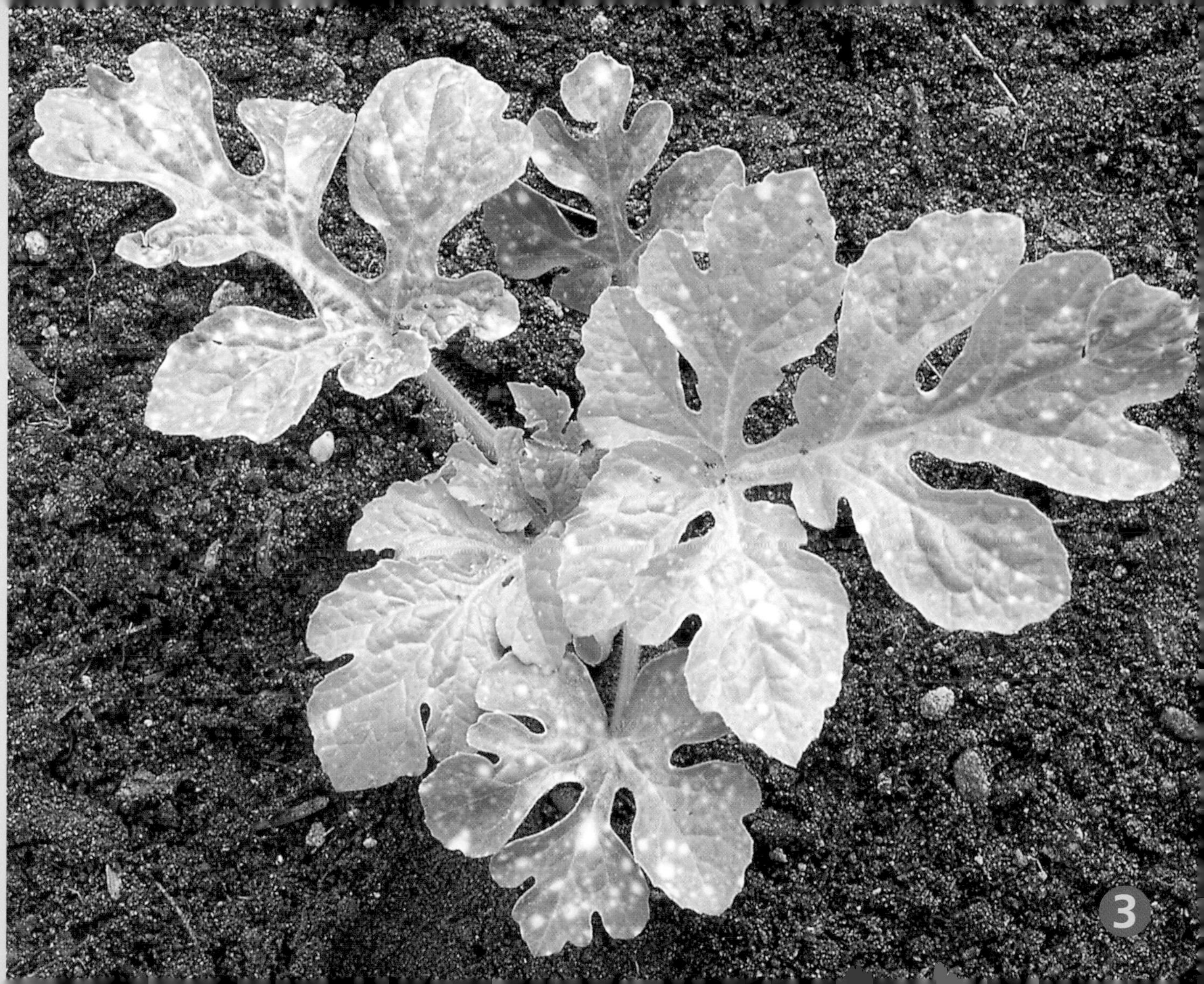
3

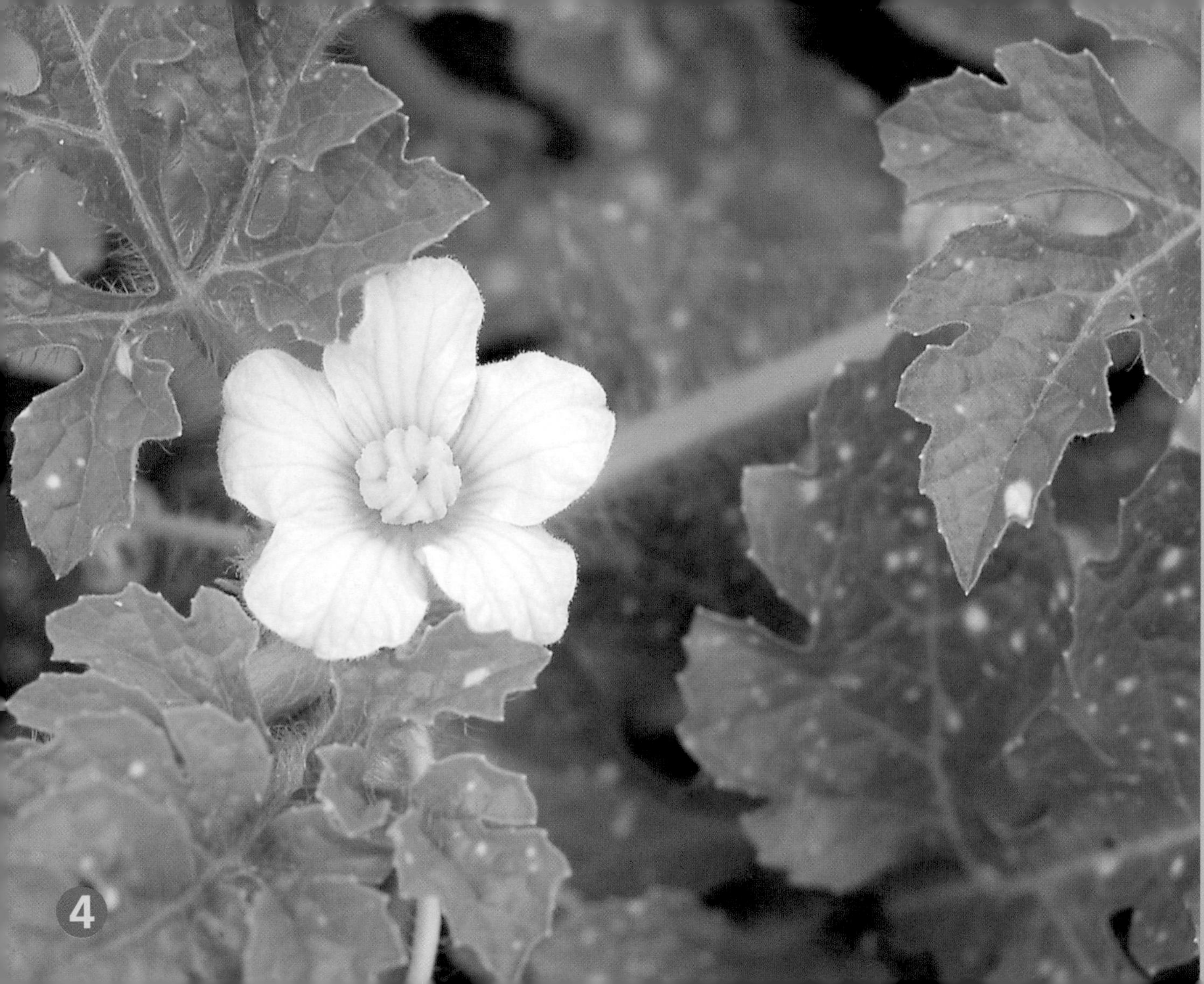

4

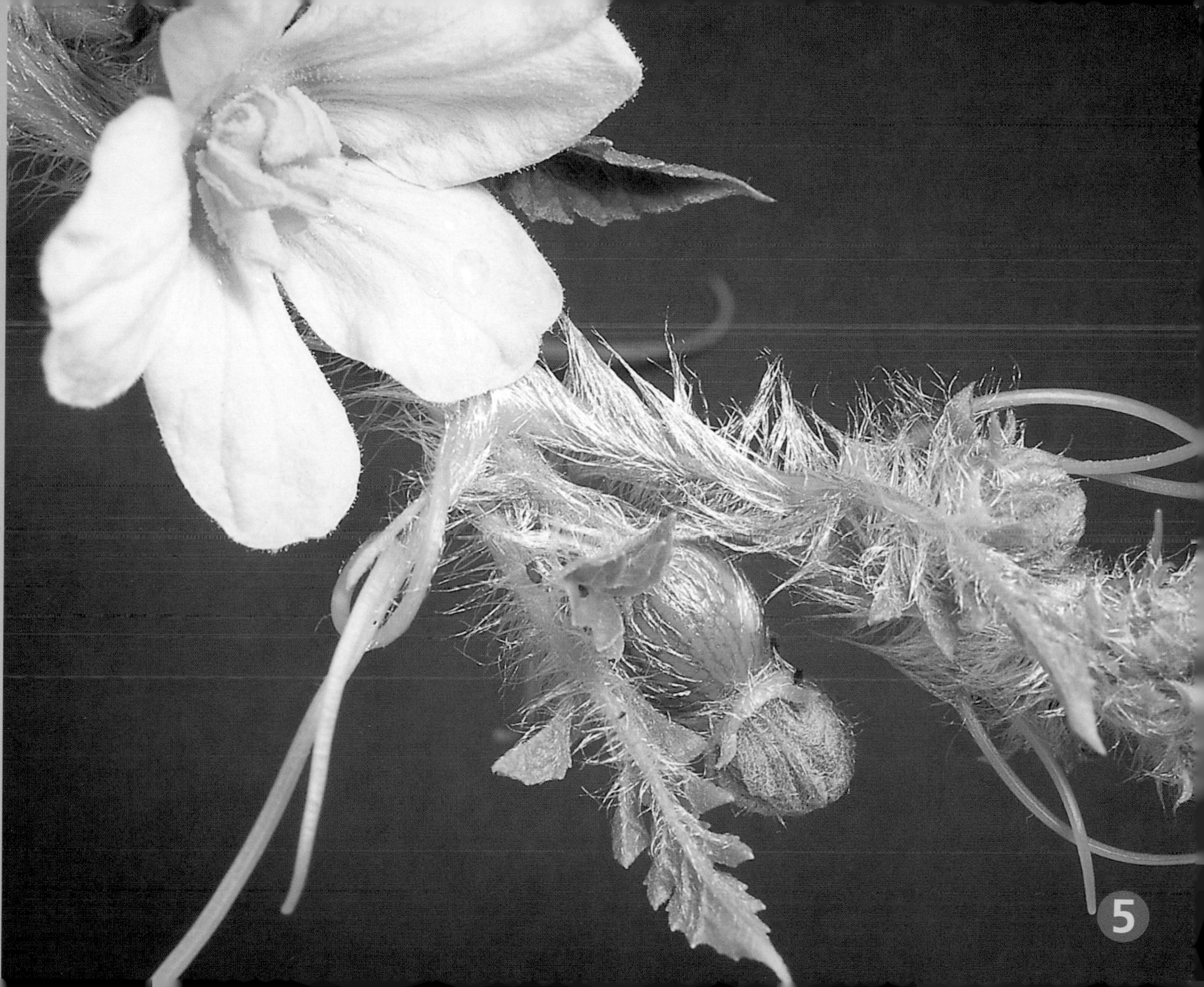
5

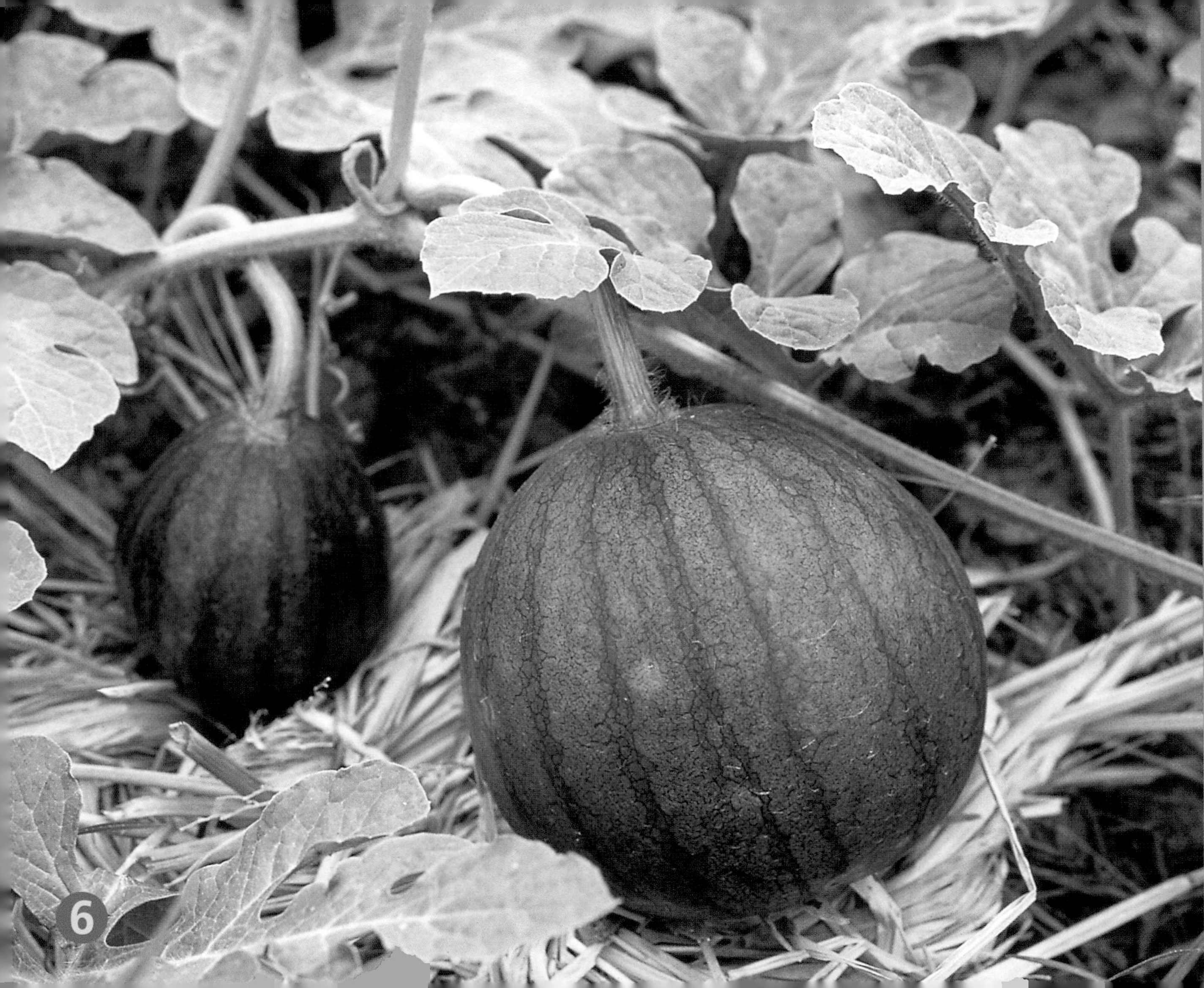
6

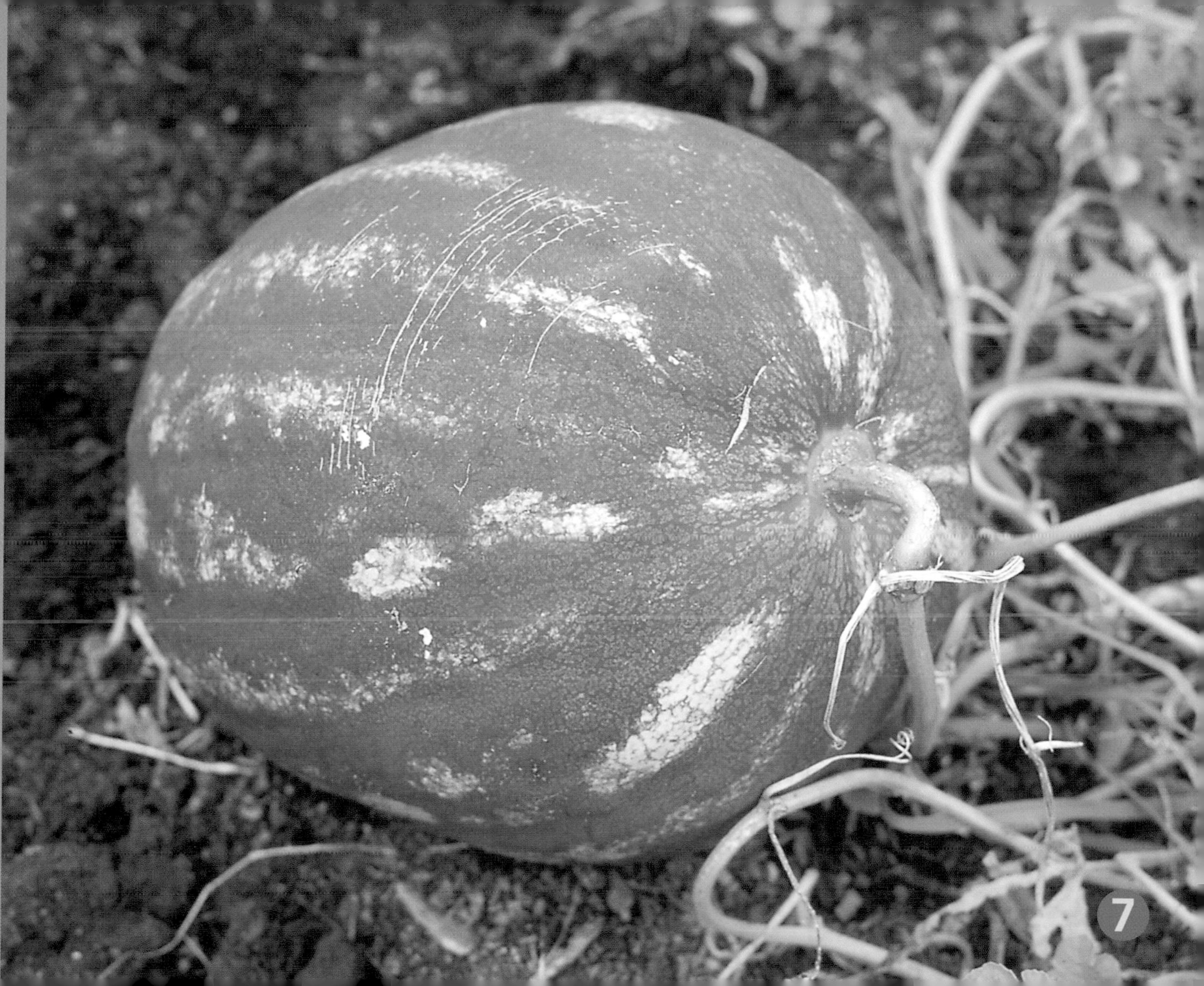
7

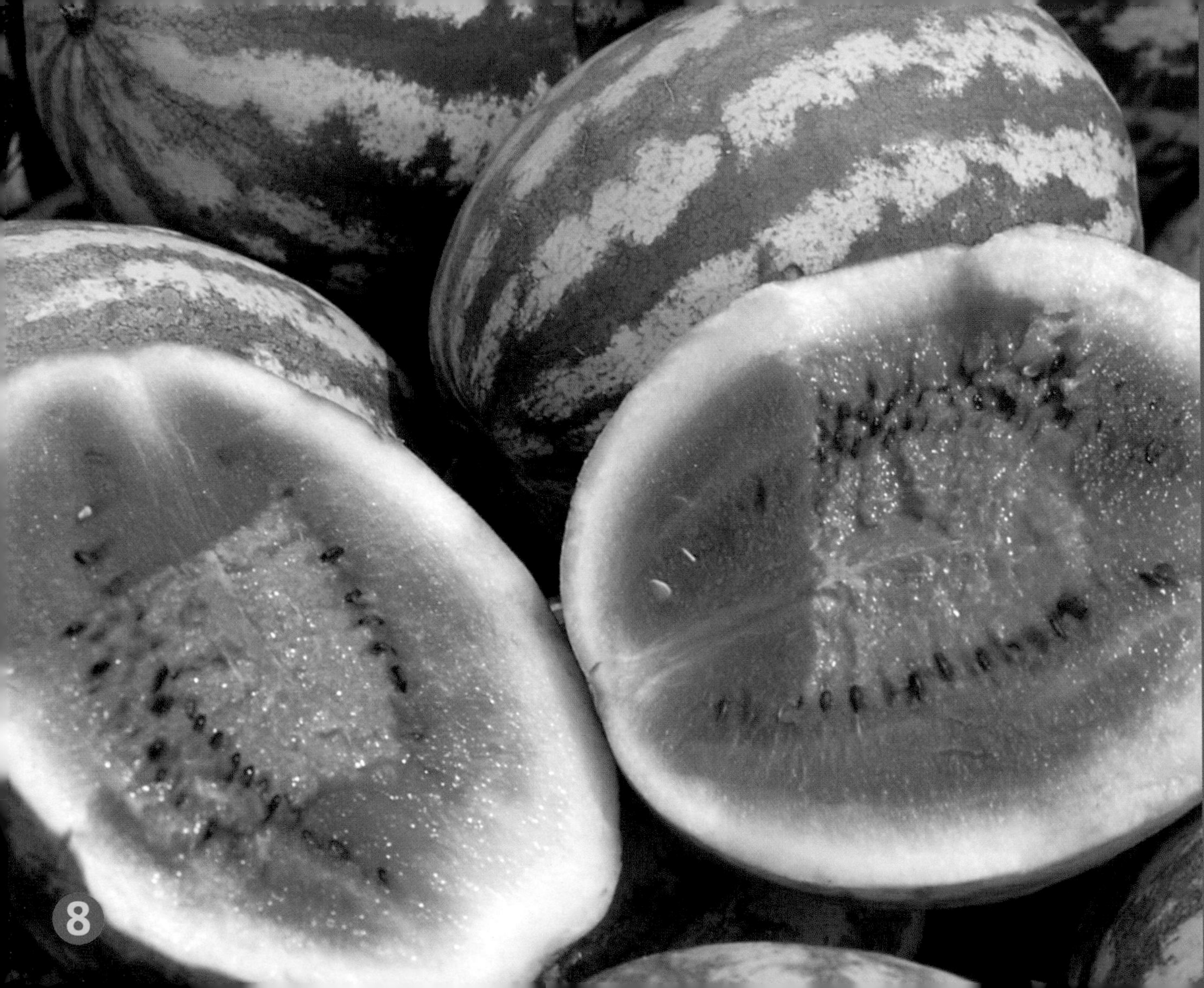